Personal Growth Book
For Women

REACHING YOUR
GREATEST FEMALE
POTENTIAL

Look No Further

JESSICA HILL

Table of Contents

Chapter 1: How Will You Choose To Live Your Life? 6
Chapter 2: There's No Time for Regrets 9
Chapter 3: Stop Setting The Wrong Goals 13
Chapter 4: Living Life Without Regrets 16
Chapter 5: It's All About Networking 18
Chapter 6: How Your Beliefs And Moods Contribute To What's Going On In Your Life 21
Chapter 7: How To Stop Feeling Overwhelmed 24
Chapter 8: How To Be Your Own Best friend 26
Chapter 9: Being 100% Happy Is Overrated 30
Chapter 10: Block Out The Critics and Detractors 33
Chapter 11: Discovering Your Purpose 36
Chapter 12: How To Live Authentically 39
Chapter 13: 7 Signs You've Outgrown your Friendship 41
Chapter 14: How To Deal With Feeling Anxious In A Relationship ... 47
Chapter 15: How To Survive a Long Distance Relationship 49
Chapter 16: Get in the Water (Stop wasting time) 54
Chapter 17: 6 Ways To Make Your Relationship Sweeter 56
Chapter 18: 7 Ways To Live Together In Harmony With Your Partner 60
Chapter 19: 5 Ways To Make New Friends Without Leaving The House 65
Chapter 20: 10 Thoughts That Can Destroy Relationships 69
Chapter 21: 9 Ways To Tell If They're Really Into You 74
Chapter 22: 6 Behaviours That Keep You Single 78
Chapter 23: 6 Ways To Be More Confident In Bed 82
Chapter 24: 6 Relationship Goals To Have 86
Chapter 25: 9 Tips on How To Have A Strong Relationship 90

Chapter 26: 8 Signs Someone Misses You 96
Chapter 27: 6 Signs You Are Emotionally Unavailable 100
Chapter 28: 7 Ways To Make Your Marriage Sweeter 104
Chapter 29: 10 Ways To Attract Love 109
Chapter 30: Ten ways men fall in Love 113
Chapter 31: 6 Signs Your Love Is One Sided.. 120

Chapter 1:

How Will You Choose To Live Your Life?

How will you choose to live your life? This is something that only you have the power to decide.

We all want different things. As individuals, we are all unique and we have our own ideas about what it means to live a meaningful life. Some treasure family, friends, and relationships above all else, while others prioritize money, material things, careers, and productivity. There is no right or wrong to pursue or place any of these things on a pedestal. If your dream is to build a multi-billion-dollar company, then go ahead and chase that dream. If you prioritize just being as stress-free as possible, to do as little work as you can, well you can choose to structure your life in such a way as well. As long as it works for you and that you are happy doing so, I would say go for it.

Sure, your priorities might change as you get older and wiser. Embrace that change. We are not always met to move in a linear fashion in life. We should learn to live like water, being fluid, ever-changing, ever-growing, ever evolving. Our interests, priorities, passions, all change as we move from one stage of life to the next.

Some only realize that they might want to focus on relationships at a certain point in their lives, some might only want to start a family when they reach a certain age. The point is that we never truly know when is the time when we might feel ready to do something, as much as well tell ourselves that we will know.

The best thing we can do for ourselves right now, in this very moment, is to do what we think is best for us right now, and then to make tweaks and adjustments along the way as we travel down that road faithfully.

Trying to plan and control every aspects of our lives rarely ever works out how we imagined it. You see, life will give us lemons, but it can also give us durians. We might get thrown off the road through unexpected changes. Things that challenge our beliefs and our priorities. Health issues, family tragedies, financial meltdowns, natural disasters, these are things that we can never plan for. We may either choose to come out of these things with a clearer plan for our next phase of life, or we may choose to give up and not try anymore.

All of us have the power to choose how we want to live our lives in this very moment. The worst thing you can do right now is not know what your priorities are and to just cruise through life without having at least a short-term vision on what you want to get out of it.

Take the time to reflect every single day to work on that goal, however scary or simple it may be. Never take your eye off the post and just keep traveling down that path until you reach a fork in the road.

Chapter 2:

There's No Time for Regrets

Regret. Guilt. Shame.

These are three of the darkest emotions any human will ever experience. We all feel these things at different points in our lives, especially after making a "bad" decision. There are certain situations some of us would rewind (or delete) if we could. The reality is, however, there is an infinite number of reasons we should never regret any of the decisions we make in our lives.

Here are 7 of them:

1. Every decision allows you to take credit for creating your own life.

Decisions are not always the result of thoughtful contemplation. Some of them are made on impulse alone. Regardless of the decision, when you made it, it was something you wanted, or you would not have done it (unless someone was pointing a gun at your head).

Be willing to own the decisions you make. Be accountable for them. Take responsibility and accept them.

2. By making any decision involving your heart, you have the chance to create more love in the world by spreading yours.

Your love is a gift.

Once you decide to love, do it without reservation. By fully giving of yourself, you expand your ability to express and receive love. You have added to the goodness of our universe by revealing your heart to it.

3. By experiencing the disappointment that might come with a decision's outcome, you can propel yourself to a new level of emotional evolution.

You aren't doing yourself any favors when you try to save yourself from disappointment. Disappointment provides you with an opportunity to redefine your experiences in life. By refining your reframing skills, you increase your resilience.

4. "Bad" decisions are your opportunity to master the art of self-forgiveness.

When you make a "bad" decision, you are the person who is usually the hardest on yourself. Before you can accept the consequences of your decision and move on, you must forgive yourself. You won't always make perfect choices in your life. Acknowledge the beauty in your human imperfection, then move forward and on.

5. Because of the occasional misstep, you enable yourself to live a Technicolor life.

Anger. Joy. Sadness. These emotions add pigment to your life. Without these things, you would feel soulless. Your life would be black and white.

Make your decisions with gusto. Breathe with fire. You are here to live in color.

6. Your ability to make a decision is an opportunity to exercise the freedom that is your birthright.

How would you feel if you had no say in those decisions concerning your life? Would you feel powerless? Restricted? Suffocated?

Now, focus on what it feels like to make the decisions you want to make. What do you feel? Freedom? Liberty? Independence? What feelings do you want to feel?

Freedom. Liberty. Independence. As luck would have it, the freedom you want is yours. Be thankful for it in every decision you make, "good" or "bad."

7. When you decide to result in ugly aftermath, you refine what you do want in your life.

It's often impossible to know what you want until you experience what you don't want. With every decision, you will experience consequences. Use those outcomes as a jumping-off point to something different (and better) in your future.

Chapter 3:

Stop Setting The Wrong Goals

Setting the wrong goals will lead to disappointment in success.
Chances are you are aiming too low and
will not be satisfied with the outcome.
The outcome and the reason for
it must be clear before you begin.
Will the result make you satisfied?
Will you enjoy the journey to the result?
Your goal should encompass these questions
to make sure you are not setting the wrong goals.

You may be setting the wrong goals due to the expectations of others.
The goals you set should be personal to you -
something where you can enjoy the process and the result.
Is your goal likely to happen based on your current actions?
What could you do to make it more likely?
If you set the wrong goals, you will end up doing a whole lot of work you
don't like doing for a result you don't want.

Start at the end in your mind.
What would the end result look, taste and feel like?

With that you can imagine the process.
Can you do that work?
Would you enjoy that work?
Or would the reality fall short of your current expectations.

Life is chess not checkers.
The grand masters of success play 10 years ahead.
Thinking about how their actions today will
influence their lives ten years from now.
What's your 10-year goal?
What are your first steps?
Start at the end and work it back to now in your mind.

If you can envision the goal and paths to it
the battle is half won and you will have clarity over your goals.
Setting the wrong goals decreases your motivation to attain them.
You can only attain your motivation if your why is strong enough.

What are you aiming for and why?
If your clarity is strong enough, you will
feel the goal as if it is already real.
You can then confirm it is the right goal for you.

If you only feel half-hearted about something it is not for you
and it is probably a waste of your time.
It's better to go all out for something you really want
than to easily obtain something you don't.

The right goal for you will probably feel unrealistic at first.
People will probably tell you it is.
But you know that it really isn't.
If it's on your mind constantly then it
stands a good chance that it is the right goal for you.

You must think clearly about every aspect of your life
and the goal you wish to obtain.
Something that fits you and your true desires.

Your goal should be something that will make you happy as often as possible and give you the kind of financial life you want.
Never set goals because someone else thinks that is what you should be doing.

Only you know what you should be doing,
go after that and never accept anything less.
Gain clarity on your goals before you act.
Make sure it's something that will make you happy in the process and the results that come from it.

Chapter 4:

Living Life Without Regrets

As Mick Jagger once said, "the past is a great place and I don't want to erase it or to regret it, but I don't want to be its prisoner either." Regret is like an uninvited ghost, and it likes to make an appearance when we are at our lowest. It dwells in the back of our heads from time to time and reminds us of the things that we wish we had done differently in our lives. But, just like a million other things and emotions, regrets only stay with us if we feed on it and let it in. It can be A heavy burden for us to carry, so in order to get rid of this lingering ghost, it's essential that we first understand what we are actually regretting and why.

If your life were about to end tomorrow - if that drunk doesn't stop at the red light, or the meteor is headed right for your house, would you go into your memory and start seeing your regrets? Or would you just accept it all and wish that you had lived your life more freely? Trust me when I say this, it's really okay to screw up. We're not people who can't make any mistakes and be flawless. Take A hurdler in the Olympics as an example; he knocks over about half of the hurdles in that 110 metres, and they don't even break stride. Because at the end, it's not about not knocking over any hurdles or running the perfect race, it all comes down to getting across the line. So don't ever fear or regret failing - you give it A shot, and that's all that matters in the end.

We all know how Michael Jordan struggled with his career. In his own words, "I've missed more than 9000 shots in my career. I've lost almost 3000 games. 26 times, I've been trusted to take the game winning shot and missed. I've failed over and over and over again in my life. And that's why I succeed." Had he given up in his first try, the world would have never known A legend like him. He must've had A thousand second thoughts every time he failed, he must've regretted opting basketball every time he lost A game, but he kept going and never gave up. We should have A similar outlook on our lives. No matter what we did in our past, or whatever our decisions were that led to what we are now, it all must have A connection or A meaning. We just have to stop, think, and analyze.

Now, the first step to explore the space of your mind and begin addressing the things that you regret, is to have A conversation with yourself. But keep in mind, this isn't A blame game and it definitely isn't meant for you to slip down into A rabbit hole of self-sabotage. Holding onto regret is one form of self-sabotaging, but you should move forward by identifying things that are working against you and having healthier conversations with yourself to get to the root of things. Regret is A powerful emotion, it can consume your thoughts, energy, and time. Feeling miserable is totally fine as long as you keep A check on yourself and don't let it drain you completely. No matter what your situation is, you can work on this "ghost of regret" to leave by starting doing positive things for yourself. Feed your life with passion and love, and regrets will say good-bye to you soon.

Chapter 5:

It's All About Networking

Networking isn't merely the exchange of information with others — and it's certainly not about begging for favors. Networking is about establishing and nurturing long-term, mutually beneficial relationships with the people you meet, whether you're waiting to order your morning coffee, participating in an intramural sports league, or attending a work conference. You don't have to join several professional associations and attend every networking event that comes your way in order to be a successful networker. In fact, if you take your eyes off your smartphone when you're out in public, you'll see that networking opportunities are all around you every day.

Experts agree that the most connected people are often the most successful. When you invest in your relationships — professional and personal — it can pay you back in dividends throughout the course of your career. Networking will help you develop and improve your skill set, stay on top of the latest trends in your industry, keep a pulse on the job market, meet prospective mentors, partners, and clients, and gain access to the necessary resources that will foster your career development.
Career development, in its simplest terms, is the lifelong evolution of your career. It's influenced by a number of things that include the jobs you hold, the experiences you gain in and out of the office, the success

you achieve at each stage of your career, the formal and informal education and training you receive, and the feedback you're provided with along the way.

Ideally, organizations would place more emphasis on employee development in the workplace. However, the reality is that we live in what Carter Cast, author of the book, "The Right (and Wrong) Stuff: How Brilliant Careers Are Made," refers to as "the era of do-it-yourself career development."

Cast explains that in today's workforce, the burden is on you to take control of your career development. Hence the importance of networking for career development: As you network with people at your company, in your industry, and even outside your field of interest, you'll uncover opportunities to connect with different types of mentors and advisors, increase your visibility with senior management, further develop your areas of expertise, and improve your soft skills. You may assume that networking is an activity reserved for your time out of the office and off the clock, but nothing could be further from the truth.

While there is much value in connecting with people who work at other companies or in different fields, don't discount the importance of networking in the workplace. Whether you're new to the company and want to get the lay of the land or you're already established and have your sights set on a promotion, networking with your co-workers can be incredibly beneficial to your career progression.

As you develop relationships with those in your department and in other divisions, be on the lookout for potential mentors, upcoming professional development opportunities, or new job opportunities that are not publicly advertised. It's never too early — or too late — to invest in your network. The best way to improve your networking skills is to put yourself out there and give it a try. According to Baikowitz, "the worst networking mistake you can make is not trying at all."

Chapter 6:

How Your Beliefs And Moods Contribute To What's Going On In Your Life

Because our ability to successfully interact with other people is so important to our survival, these skills have become part of human nature. We determine whether to help in large part on the basis of how other people make us feel, and how we think we will feel if we help or do not help them.

Positive Moods Increase, Helping

I do not need to tell you that people help more when they are in good mood. We ask our parents to use their car, and we ask our boss for a raise, when we think they are in a positive mood rather than a negative one. Positive moods have been shown to increase many types of helping behavior, including contributing to charity, donating blood, and helping coworkers (isen, 1999). It is also relatively easy to put people in a good mood. You might not be surprised to hear that people are more likely to help after they've done well on a test or just received a big bonus in their paycheck. But research has found that even more trivial things, such as finding a coin in a phone booth, listening to a comedy recording, having someone smile at you, or even smelling the pleasant scent of perfume is enough to put people in a good mood and to cause them to be helpful (baron & thomley, 1994; gueguen & de gail, 2003; isen & levin, 1972).

In another study, van baaren, holland, kawakami, and van knippenberg (2004) had students interact with an experimenter who either mimicked them by subtly copying their behaviors outside of their awareness or did not mimic them. The researchers found that people who had been mimicked were more likely to help, by picking up pens that had fallen on the floor and by donating to a charity. It is quite possible that this effect is due to the influence of positive moods on helping—we like people we see as similar to us and that puts us in a good mood, making us more likely to help. In sum, the influence of mood on helping is substantial (carlson, charlin, & miller, 1988), so if you're looking for help, ask on a nice day, subtly mimic the person's behaviors, or prepare some good jokes.

But why does being in a good mood make us helpful? There are probably several reasons. For one, a positive mood indicates that the environment is not dangerous and therefore that we can safely help others. Second, we like other people more when we are in good moods, and that may lead us to help them. Finally, and perhaps most important, is the possibility the helping makes us feel good about ourselves, thereby maintaining our positive mood. In fact, people who are in good moods are particularly likely to help when the help that they are going to give seems likely to maintain their positive mood. But if they think that the helping is going spoil their good mood, even people in good moods are likely to refuse to help (erber & markunas, 2006).

In the end, we cannot completely rule out the possibility that people help in large part for selfish reasons. But does it really matter? If we give money to the needy because we will feel bad about ourselves if we do not, or if we give money to the needy because we want them to feel good, we have nevertheless made the contribution in both cases.

Chapter 7:

How To Stop Feeling Overwhelmed

There might come a million instances in your life when you will feel overwhelmed. Whether it's college, work, social obligations, family, or life in general, life can get anxious, stressed, and overwhelmed at certain times. It's important to recognize these feelings and give yourself grace when you have these feelings. Try to dive deeper into your emotions and understand what's causing them, don't brush them off or push through whatever's causing you to feel anxious. Your mental health matters more than anything, and if you're feeling the squeeze, know that you can always take a step back.

When things start to feel a little too much for you, take a deep breath and step away. If you feel anxious or overwhelmed, start doing some breathing exercises to alleviate those feelings. If the thing that's causing you anxiety is right in front of you, take a step away from it and create some separation between you that's overwhelming you. Deep breathing exercises will promote relaxation and would lower your stress response immediately. Understand that we all go through these phases, and it's completely okay and normal to feel like this. Cut yourself some slack and be kind towards yourself. If you're unable to do that chore or have to ask for some extension in your deadline, then do that. Your mental health should be your top priority.

While most of the time, we might want to get isolated or want everyone to leave us alone in our times of stress and anxiety, it's better to reach out to a loved one and ask for their support and help. You can also virtually chat to an online psychologist and rant to them to feel better. Or you can pick up the phone and call your friends or family and ask for their comfort and consolation.

You can also find a hobby that you find relaxation in. It can either be swimming, driving, baking, reading, or any of the stuff that calms your mind, and you enjoy doing it. Writing down your reasons for anxiousness and being overwhelmed can also be a great way to alleviate those feelings. It helps you express yourself freely and provides a sense of relief once all of those thoughts are out of your head. Always remember that whatever you're feeling is temporary. With the right coping mechanisms and support, you can always take care of yourself when things start to go south. Protect your time and space and create healthy boundaries for yourself.

Chapter 8:
How To Be Your Own Best Friend

Why would you want to become your own best friend? There are several benefits to creating your internal support system rather than relying on your partner, friends, or family to be there for you when you're suffering. Having other people's expectations can lead to disappointment, heartbreak, and relationship breakdown if your expectations aren't met.

We all have it in us to give ourselves what we need without seeking it externally.

Of course, it's great if you have a strong support network, but you could still benefit from becoming more self-reliant. And what about if you have no one to turn to for help, or if your current support people are unable to be there for you?
Isn't it far better to know how to support yourself in times of need?

Here's how to become your own best friend.

1. Be Nice To Yourself

The first step to becoming a friend is to treat yourself like you would treat a friend. That means that you need to stop being self-critical and beating yourself up. Start by acknowledging your good qualities, talents, and abilities and begin to appreciate your unique self.
When you catch yourself thinking up some nasty self-talk, stop and ask, "Would I say this to my best friend?" If not, then reframe your self-talk to be more supportive and caring.

2. Imagine How You Would Support A Friend In The Same Situation

Think about a loved one, a friend, a family member, someone dear to you and imagine that they are in the same situation you are currently facing. Think about how they're struggling, suffering, and feeling stuck with this problem, then consider how to best offer assistance and advice to them.

Craft the words that you would say to your greatest friend and then say them gently to yourself. Allow yourself to feel supported and give yourself what you need.

3. Honor Your Needs

Following the theme of considering how you would help a dear friend, you need to start taking your advice and putting your own needs first. Do you need a day off from work? A long hot bath? An early night? A wild night? Some time to catch up on your reading, cleaning, gardening, creative projects, social life, or self-care?

Whatever you need, allow yourself to put it at the top of the list rather than the bottom. Be there for yourself and make it happen.

4. Send Compassion To The Part of You That is Hurting

Being a friend to yourself involves adopting and mastering the art of self-compassion. Compassion isn't forceful or solution focused. Compassion is accepting, peaceful, and loving, without the need to control or change anything.

Imagine a mother holding a child who has bumped his head. Her compassion is a strong force. She simply holds her child with loving, comforting, gentle arms and whispers, "It will be alright, my love." The child trusts his mother's words just as you learn to trust your own words when speaking to yourself.

Imagine yourself as both the child and the mother simultaneously. Offer compassion at the same time as you open up to receive it.

Use these techniques to become your own best friend and start being there for yourself!

Chapter 9:

Being 100% Happy Is Overrated

Lately I've been feeling as though happiness isn't something that truly lasts. Happiness isn't something that will stay with us very long. We may feel happy when we are hanging out with friends, but that feeling will eventually end once we part for the day. I've been feeling as though expecting to be constantly happy is very overrated. We try to chase this idea of being happy. We chase the material possessions, we chase the fancy cars, house, and whatever other stuff that we think will make us happy. But more often than not the desire is never really fulfilled. Instead, i believe that the feeling accomplishment is a much better state of mind to work towards. Things will never make us happy. We may enjoy the product we have worked so hard for temporarily. But that feeling soon goes away. And we are left wondering what is the next best thing we can aim our sights on. This never-ending chase becomes a repetitive cycle, one that we never truly are aware of but constantly desire. We fall into the trap that finding happiness is the end all-be-all.

What I've come to realize is that most of the time, we are actually operating on a more baseline level. A state that is skewed more towards the neutral end. Neither truly happy, nor neither truly sad. And I believe that is perfectly okay. We should allow ourselves to embrace and accept the fact that it is okay to be just fine. Just neutral. Sure, it isn't something very exciting, but we shouldn't put ourselves in a place where we expect to be constantly happy in order to lead a successful life. This revelation came when I realized that every time I felt happy, I would experience a crash in mood the next day. I would start looking at Instagram, checking up on my friends, comparing their days, and thinking that they are leading a happier life than I was. I would then start berating myself and find ways to re-create those happy moments just for the sake of it. Just because I thought i needed to feel happy all the time. It was only when I actually sat down and started looking inwards did I realize that maybe I can never truly find happiness from external sources.

Instead of trying to find happiness in things and external factors that are beyond my control, I started looking for happiness from within myself. I began to appreciate how happy I was simply being alone. Being by myself. Not letting other factors pull me down. I found that I was actually happiest when I was taking a long shower, listening to my own thoughts. No music playing, no talking to people, just me typing away on my computer, writing down all the feelings I am feeling, all the thoughts that I am thinking, letting every emotion I was feeling out of my system. I started to realize that the lack of distractions, noise, comparisons with others, free from social media, actually provided me with a clearer mind. It was in those brief moments where I found myself to be my most productive, with ideas streaming all over the place. It was in that state of mind that I did feel somewhat happy. That I could create that state of mind without depending on other people to fulfil it for me.

If any of you out there feel that your emotions are all over the place, maybe it is time for you to sit down by yourself for a little while. Stop searching for happiness in things and stuff, and sometimes even people. We think it is another person's job to make us happy. We expect to receive compliments, flowers, a kiss, in order to feel happy. While those things are certainly nice to have, being able to find happiness from within is much better. By sitting and reflecting in a quiet space, free from any noise and distractions, we may soon realize that maybe we are okay being just okay. Maybe we don't need expensive jewelry or handbags or fancy houses to make us happy. Maybe we just need a quiet mind and a grateful spirit.

The goal is to find inner peace. To accept life for the way it is. To accept things as the way they are. To be grateful for the things we have. That is what it means to be happy.

Chapter 10:

Block Out The Critics and Detractors

There is drama everywhere around us. In fact, our whole life is a drama. A drama that has more complex turns and thrillers than the best thriller ever to be made on a cinema screen.

This drama isn't always a result of our own actions. Sometimes we do something stupid to contribute towards anarchy. But mostly the things happening around us seem to be a drama because the critics make a hell out of everything.

We get sucked into things that and someone else's opinions because we do not know what we are doing.

It may sound cliche but remember that it doesn't matter what anyone else says. In fact, most discoveries and inventions got bad press when they were found or made. It was only after they are gone when people actually came to appreciate the true importance of those inventions.

The time will come sooner or later when you are finally appreciated for your work and your effort. But your work should not depend on what others will say.

Your work should not depend on the hope of appreciation or the fear of criticism, rather it should be done because it was meant to be done. You should put your heart and soul in it because you had a reason for all this and only you will reap the fruit, no matter what the world gets from it.

You don't need to do the best out there in the world and neither should you be judged on that standard. But you should put out the best YOU can do because that will someday shut out the critics as they start to see your true potential.

The work itself doesn't matter, but the effort you put behind it does. You don't need to be an insult to anyone who mocks you or criticizes you on even your best work. Empathy is your best approach to bullying.

You cannot possibly shut out every critic. You spend your whole life trying to answer to those meaningless least important people that weren't even able to make their own lives better. Because those who did make something of themselves didn't find it worthwhile to distract and degrade everyone else.

So, you should try to spend your time more and more on your good work. Keep a straight sight without even thinking to look at one more ordinary critic who doesn't give a simple feeling of empathy towards your efforts.

You only need to put yourself in others' shoes and look at yourself through their eyes. If you can do that before them, you would have the best reply to any hurtful comment. And that my friend will be true silence.

People always come to gather around you when they see a cause they can relate to. So, give them a cause. Give a ray of hope and motivation to people around you and you will finally get to get the critics on your side.

Your critics will help you get to the top from the hardest side there is.

Chapter 11:

Discovering Your Purpose

If you guys don't already know, this is one of the topics that I really love talking about. And I never get tired of it. Having a purpose is something that I always believe everyone should have. Having a purpose to live, to breathe, to get up each day, I believe that without purpose, there is no point to life.

So today we're going to talk about how to discover your purpose, and why you should make it a point to find one if you didn't already start looking.

So, what is purpose exactly. A purpose is a reason to do something. Is to have something else greater than ourselves to work for. You see, I believe if we are only focused on ourselves, instead of others, we will not be able to be truly happy in life. Feeding our own self interests does not bring us joy as one might think. After living the life that I had, I realized that true happiness only comes when you bring joy to someone else's life. Whether it be helping others professionally or out of selflessness, this happiness will radiate and reflect back to us from someone else who is appreciative of your efforts.

On some level, we can look into ourselves to be happy. For example, being grateful for life, loving ourselves, and all that good stuff. Yes, keep doing those things. But there is a whole other dimension if we devote our time and energy into helping others once we have already conquered ourselves. If you look at many of the most successful people on the planet, after they have acquired an immense amount of wealth, many of them look to passion projects or even philanthropy where they can give back to the community when having more money doesn't do anything for them anymore. If you look at Elon Musk and Jeff Bezos, these two have a greater purpose which is their space projects. Where they visualize humans being able to move out of Earth one day where civilization is able to expand. Or Bill Gates and Warren Buffet, who have pledged to give billions of their money away for philanthropic work, to help the less fortunate and to fund organizations that work towards finding cures to diseases.

Now for us mere mortals, we don't need to think so big. Our purpose need not be so extravagant. It can be as simple as having a purpose to provide for your loved one, to work hard to bring your family members of holidays and travel, or to bring joy to your elderly relatives by organizing activities for them to do. There is no purpose that is too big or too small.

Your purpose could be helping others find a beautiful home, doing charitable work, or even feeding and providing for your growing family.

As humans, we will automatically work harder if we have a clear and defined purpose. We have a reason to get up each day, to go to work, to earn that paycheck, so that we can spend it on things and people, even ourselves at times. Without a purpose, we struggle to find meaning in the work that we do. We struggle to see the big picture and we find that we have no reason to work so hard, or even at all. And we struggle to find life worth living.

This revelation came to me when I started seeing my work as helping some other person in a meaningful way. Where my work was not just about making money to buy nice things, but to be able to impact someone else's life in a positive way. That became my purpose. To see them learn something new, and to bring a joy and smile to their faces. That thought that I was contributing something useful to someone made me smile more than money ever could. Yes money can help you live a comfortable life, but helping others can go a much farther way into giving your life true purpose.

So, I challenge each and everyone of you to find a purpose in everything that you do, and if you struggle to find one, start by making the goal to help others a priority. Think of the difference you can make to others and that could very well be your purpose in life as well.

Chapter 12:

How To Live Authentically

What does being authentic mean? How do I know if the life I'm leading is authentic? Am I happy with the person I've become? Finally, is authenticity overrated? And if you're anything like me, your train of thought maybe similar. It's easy to forget how to be authentic when we play many different roles throughout the day. We're parents, children, friends, employees, teachers, lovers, members of society. But how do we stay true to ourselves when life gets messy, overwhelming, or stressful? By taking small steps and doing little things that make us feel good. No, scratch that. That makes us feel great. Excellent. Ecstatic. Alive. Grateful for who we are and what we have. But also calm, meditative, reflective. I made a shortlist of simple things that have helped me live more authentically and be closer to my genuine self.

1. Enjoy The Little Things

I know – this is a cliché, but I can't deny this simple truth. In all honesty, it can take some practice to train your mind to stop blabbering and start noticing the little things. But once it does, you will. Rejoice in the first rays of sunshine on a hazy morning. Feel their warmth on your skin. Smell that first cup of coffee and exhale with a sigh of blissful pleasure as you take that first sip. Hug your pet. Kiss your loved one. Have fresh flowers on your table. Listen to the ocean. Watch the sunset. Let the wind blow through your hair in the spring. Walk on crispy leaves in the fall. Make snow angels in the winter. You know, the little things. Every day, I make conscious efforts to appreciate and remember the special moments and people in my life.

2. Don't Judge or Punish Yourself for Your Mistakes

We often think it's ok to judge ourselves for a mistake we've made either now or in the past. But what's the use? Instead of beating yourself up, see if you can learn something from your failures. So, what helps is writing down what each of your mistakes is trying to teach you and how you can avoid repeating it in the future. But please, don't judge yourself. You did the best you could do.

Sometimes, you'll find your true self with life experience and maturity. Other times, it may be hidden under anxiety and depression, feelings of inadequacy, negative self-talk, self-doubt, and fear. And finding it may take some therapy. But the authentic self has no high expectations of themselves or others and takes life lightly. Instead of constantly doing, running, working, thinking – it just is. Innocent and vulnerable, but also strong and independent. For me, authenticity equals freedom. So tell me – what does authenticity mean to you? How do you find it? Do you have any tips to add to this list? I'd love to hear your thoughts in the comments below.

Chapter 13:

7 Signs You've Outgrown your Friendship

Growing up, we have always listened to the phrase "friendships last forever." And while some of them may do, some are just destined to end with time. It's difficult to say goodbye to someone with whom you spend a very long time and have a lot of history together. All those years of laughing hysterically on the inside jokes, making fun memories, and offering a shoulder to cry on whenever one of the two of you were struggling, putting an end to these might be more painful than you have thought so.

As children, we felt that our friends wouldn't ever change, and everything would remain just the same. But as it turns out, adulthood brings a significant amount of change into everyone's lives. As a result, our interests and priorities often diverge wildly when we enter our 20s and 30s, and by then, we start realizing that some of our friends might not be a good fit for us. And it's not because we have started to dislike them or did something unforgivable, instead because we have all simply changed.

Losing the thread of connection with a close friend can sometimes be more heart-breaking than ending a romantic relationship. But your well-being needs to acknowledge when a friendship has run its course.

Here are a few signs that you've outgrown your friendship.

1. Your Interactions Feel Draining

If you get a sinking feeling in the pit of your stomach after you've made plans with them, rather than looking forward to it and thinking you would have a great time, then maybe it's time to reconsider the relationship with your friend. You may feel like whenever you two meet, the conversation focuses upon them, or they might bring up the topics you have little to no interest in. After hanging out with them, you feel emotionally drained, exhausted, and wrung out. You find them always complaining about their job or their relationship and asks you to listen to them and support them regardless. You're left feeling frustrated and angry and may vent to your other friends about this. These friendships tend to take more than they give and should eventually be ended.

2. You Have Nothing in Common Anymore

Your conversations will be filled with awkwardness or constant arguments if you don't have anything in common with them. As communication is the key to maintain any relationship, having nothing to talk about would make you two feel bored, and the conversations would feel strained and unnatural. Maybe you two bonded over a shared interest that now seems childish and stupid. Eventually, your friendship would end because of the lack of substance in the relationship. People grow and people change, it could just be that you've outgrown your current friendship with the person.

3. You're the Only One Putting Efforts

You might feel that your friendship has become one-sided. You're the only one that's making sure to make plans and follow them up. You find yourself constantly checking up on them, being there for them in their good and their bad, congratulating them on their successes, and offering them their shoulder in crisis. But you see them constantly giving excuses not to make or cancel plans. You don't see them putting the same effort and consideration when it comes to you. It's like you are the only one who's working hard to make the friendship last. You're either requesting them or mocking them to put more effort, but the other person either will not or cannot comply. It is frustrating when the other party does not reciprocate. Maybe their lives have become so busy and you are no longer a priority to them. In that case, consider just letting this friendship drop by the wayside and move on to others who want to make time for you.

4. They're Constantly Judging and Criticizing You

In a healthy friendship, you wouldn't mind taking some honest criticism from your friends. After all, who knows us better than our friends? But if the complaint becomes constant and starts affecting your mental health, know that the friendship has become toxic. If your friend judges you on something that you've told them or brings you down by making fun of you in front of everyone, or becomes jealous of your successes, then it's time for you to put an end to it. If you feel the negative energy whenever you're with them and ends up being more upset than happy, then it's a sign that maybe you've outgrown that friendship.

5. You've Formed New Friendships

You've made new friends with whom you share similar goals, ask them for mature advice, or simply rely on them in your tough times. They support you throughout it all and help you deal with your career, family, and relationships. You find yourself wishing that your old friends could be more like them. But we can't change people. We have to accept that they are no longer the right fit for us, and maybe it's time for us to move on from the friendship.

6. You're in Different Phases of Your Life

As the quote goes, "People come into your life for a reason, a season, or a lifetime." The most bittersweet end to a friendship would be if you're in different seasons of your lives and have started to drift apart slowly. Maybe you're going away for college, and they're still there living with their family. Or perhaps they are getting engaged, and you have just gone through a breakup. Maybe you have found a new job while they're still struggling to graduate. Perhaps you have found the meaning of your life in a different light while they're still stuck on the same page. Whatever it is, it's just an inevitable part of life that you might not be syncing up with the phase that they are in.

7. You've started to see them as Immature and Childish

There was a time when their immature acts would look adorable to you. Now, they get on your nerves. They have started to cross all the boundaries, and when you confront them, they mask it with "I was just having fun with you." You two once shared the same sense of humor, but now your ideas and views have become different and aren't funny. They might joke about your insecurities, say hurtful and offensive things, and then becomes upset with you that you can't take a joke. Friends shouldn't drain your energy like this. They should support you and respect your boundaries and space, rather than violating them.

Conclusion

No matter what stage or age you are in your life, remember that you are a free person. You shouldn't feel obliged to continue any relationship that threatens your mental peace and energy. Friends may fade, but the memories you made with them will live in your heart forever. Sure, it might be excruciatingly painful for the both of you to end the friendship, but you must do so maturely and on good terms. It's best to let the person go with whom you've outgrown your friendship and focus on the following aspects of your life.

Chapter 14:

How To Deal With Feeling Anxious In A Relationship

There are different ways in which relationship anxiety can show up. A lot of people, when they are forming a commitment or when they are in the early stages of their relationship, feel a little insecure now; this is not something we would consider unusual, so if you have doubts or fears, you don't need to worry if they are not affecting you a lot. But sometimes, what happens is that these doubts and anxious thoughts creep into your day-to-day life. We will list some of the signs of relationship anxiety so you can figure them out for yourself, and then we will tell you how to deal with them.

1. Wondering if you matter to your partner
2. Worrying they want to breakup
3. Doubting your partners feeling for you
4. Sabotaging the relationship

These are some of the signs of relationship anxiety; now, it can take time to get to the roots of what is causing this. Right now, we will tell you how you can overcome it; yes, you read that right, you can overcome it no matter how hard it feels like at the moment. However, it will take time and consistent effort. The first thing you should do is manage anxiety early as soon as you see the symptoms because you keep delaying it. It will become a problem for you. What will help you is maintaining your identity. When you and your partner start getting closer, you will shift the key parts of your identity to make room for your partner and the relationship. You need to know that this does not help either of you. You will lose yourself, and your partner will lose the person they fell in love with. Secondly, practice good communication. If there is something specific, they are doing that is fuelling your anxiety, whether it's not making their bed after they wake up or spending a lot of time on their phone, talk to them about it and try to be non-accusatory and respective about also use I statement these can be a huge help during such conversations. If you feel like things are getting out of control and you will not handle them on your own, talk to a therapist that will get you some clarity. Because it's a relationship issue, try talking to a therapist that works with couples because that can be particularly helpful for you, so if you both have any underlying needs, the therapist will be able to communicate that in a better way.

Chapter 15:

How To Survive a Long Distance Relationship

Today we're going to talk about a very touchy yet important subject. If you have a partner who's not local, or you know that they are going to move countries someday, you've got to be prepared for that time to come. You've got to be sure whether you will begin a long distance relationship or whether you will move to that country to be with that person.

For the purpose of this video, I am going to assume that you have already committed to being in a long distance relationship. And as with any commitment, you have got to be willing to make compromises and sacrifices to maintain that relationship.

There are a couple of things that you will have to mentally prepare yourself for if you are in it for the long haul with this person. They could be gone for days, weeks, months, or even years. First of all, you have to ask yourself, are you okay with seeing this person only once every few months? Will you be happy if you won't be able to spend majority of the time with the person throughout the year? How will you cope with the distance? Are you okay with not having physical intimacy with the person? Will you be willing to sacrifice your freedom to wait for this person to return? And can you trust this person to be faithful to you as you spend all your time apart?

For me personally, I was committed to a long distance relationship once before. And it was the hardest thing for me to do. Especially when it came time at the airport for the send off.

Having already known prior that it would happen someday, i still went ahead with the relationship. All was well and all was fun, but time soon caught up with us and before i knew it, it was already time to say goodbye... temporarily at least. I must admit that it was tough... It was tough because we have gotten so used to spending time together physically in the same space for so long, that this sudden transition was all foreign territory to me. Not being able to touch each other, not being able to meet up for meals, not being able to just hang out at the movies, and not to mention the time zone difference. These were all very real challenges. And they were incredible hard especially in the first few months. I cried at the airport, I cried on the drive home, I was incredibly unhappy, and I was not prepared in any capacity whatsoever to feel this way. You never really know how to feel about something until it actually happens to you.

Knowing that the next time we would see each other would be months away, there was no way to know how to feel or act when suddenly it feels like a limb has been chopped off and you are just struggling to find your feet again. I looked to friends for social support and that was the thing that got me through the toughest periods. Sure, we could still FaceTime and call and whatever. Especially in this day and age, but it was still tough having a relationship over the computer. It does feel like on some level you're dating virtually. Everything had to change, and I had to relearn what it meant to be in a relationship all over again. I wasn't ever a sappy or clingy boyfriend. I know that about myself. But I do have an expectation to meet up maybe once or twice in a week. Now it's once or twice a year. And it's not fun at all.

So now I put that question back to you, after hearing this part of the story, are you willing to put yourself through this? Or would it be easier if you just chose someone who is in the same physical space with you with no plans on leaving town. If you were to ask me, I might actually do it all over again with someone like that.

The next thing that you've got to have to survive a long distance relationship, is to have a strong social support group. A group of friends that you can share your troubles with. People who can empathize with you, and people who can spend time with you in lieu of your partner. You never want to be in a situation where your partner is your entire world, because when they leave, you will most likely crumble. If you relied on them for all your happiness, their sudden absence will certainly leave you devastated. If u do not have a strong support network of friends, i would suggest you think doubly hard about committing to a long distance relationship.

Now comes the most important part, in my opinion, of having a successful long distance relationship. And that is trust. Trust in each other to be faithful, and trust in each other to do the right thing at all times.

I will bring back to my experience with my long distance relationship. To keep things short, after about a year into my LDR, I discovered that my partner had been cheating on me many times over. And my whole world did come crashing down. Having thought that everything was going according to plan up until that point, I was completely blindsided by the avalanche that hit me. It really hit me hard. But I knew that i loved myself more, and so I packed my bags and flew back home from the trip.

Getting over the relationship was relatively easy because i knew there was nothing left there anymore. There was no more trust to come home to. I had no faith in the relationship anymore and it was effectively over for me. It may sound too easy watching this video but trust me i went through a great deal and I was incredibly happy with my decision. I learned that i was incredibly resilient and that even though things didn't work out the way i had hoped, and even though my vision of the future was changed drastically, it didn't knock me down. And I chose myself first.

So my question that I put to you now is, to what extent do you trust your partner to be faithful to you? Has he or she cheated on you before? Have they always chosen you first? Can you touch your heart and say they will never do anything to hurt you? Or are you too naive like I was to believe that all is well? Because I was incredibly confident at one point that we were making the LDR work beautifully. Until it suddenly didn't. Would you be okay if you found out that your partner was cheating on you secretly overseas while you guys were apart? Would you be paranoid of the things he could do? If you can answer these things honestly, then u might be able to LDR make it work for you. If not, again, do reconsider your relationship now.

For me personally, if you don't know my stance by now, I absolutely do not believe in LDR. Especially if it's a permanent period. If your partner is gone maybe for a 3-6 month work trip. Yeah, maybe that's doable, but if they are gone for 5-6 years and if there's a big question mark behind that... I would totally back away. It would be a deal breaker for me.

The thing with relationships is that I believe it is the physical presence, the physical connection, the physical communication, and the physical touch that keeps two people together. Without any of these things on a regular basis, it is likely that a couple with drift apart on some level... And without these things, one might be tempted to seek comfort and physical intimacy elsewhere if they can't wait another 5 months before they can see you again.

But if your foundation is incredibly strong, if you guys have made a commitment, if you guys trust each other completely, and if you believe that your relationship can weather any storm, then I already think that you know you can handle a long distance relationship. I am simply here to affirm to you what you already know.

But take me as a word of warning that even strong relationships do fail in the face of a long distance relationship. So, you have to be prepared to handle anything that comes your way.

I hope I have been able to shed some light into this topic for you.

Take care and I'll see you in the next one.

Chapter 16:

Get in the Water
(Stop wasting time)

Stop wasting time.

If you have something to do, then do it. It is literally that simple. Nobody likes something hanging over their head, it is stressful and pressurising and the longer you leave it, the more of a challenge it is going to be. Just get it done.

It's like getting into cold water. You can start by dipping your big toe in, then walking away and reconsidering, before putting all five of them in, maybe if you are feeling frisky, you'll put in your whole foot. It is such a waste. You know you are going to get in the water eventually so you might as well dive in. Otherwise, you will spend 80% of your time drawing out an adjustment that could literally take a few seconds. What is the point? Just dive in and get it over with. Does it take a bigger first-off effort, yes. But it saves you so much time and energy afterwards. After the initial shock and a few seconds of feeling like your skin is trying to shrivel up, you are fine.

If we can do it with cold water then we can do it with that email, project or book. You can dive right into all that research you need to do. Yes, it seems overwhelming, and that first leap is going to be full of questions and discomfort. Mid-air you will probably be asking what you got yourself into but the great thing is that you can't stop mid-air. There's no turning around and floating on the air until you reach solid ground again. You are committed now.

The powerful thing is that 90% percent of your problem is inertia. It is that first step. It's sitting down, firing up your laptop and starting to work. It is getting past the idea that you have so much work to do and just focussing on what you can do right now. But when it comes down it you must realise that there is no work around for that. You cannot not do that first step. Even if it is just a passion you know that passion is going to keep burning you up on the inside until you allow it to burst out. There's no getting past the cold water, there is only getting into it. So you might as well jump. If you are trying to write a book, then sit down and just start typing. Even if you are not even typing words, just sit down for 25 minutes and type away at your keyboard. Then, while you are typing you will realise that you are sitting down and pressing the keys anyways so they may as well say something that make sense. I don't care if what you type is cliché because at this point, we are not worried about quality. I don't care how good your form is in your butterfly stroke if you are not even in the water. You just need to get started so that you are moving. And once you are moving you can maximise on your momentum.

Chapter 17:

6 Ways To Make Your Relationship Sweeter

Being in love is the most beautiful thing ever for some of us. Everything seems bright and colorful. You feel happy all the time, and the things you once hated seem good enough to try. However, everything takes time. When you both grow together and get to know each other better, it takes a lot of time. And of course, having strong feelings for each other is necessary for a relationship. A relationship is a way of loving someone openly and keeping someone your priority by your own free will and being someone else's priority too.

Relationships are sweet on their own. There is not much hard work needed when you are naturally and effortlessly in love with each other. Even though there are countless ways, you can dial a notch up and make your relationship even more robust, healthier, and sweeter than before. It takes a lot of time to manage everything, but love is worth it when you are with the right person. All the work and compromises seem worth it. Once you are with your charming prince and your dream princess, everything other than that is just a piece of cake. Following are some ways to make your relationship even sweeter.

1. Go On A Date Occasionally

Going on a date with the one that you love is highly romantic and sweet. It's essential to keep that spark alive between the two of you, and a date might be a perfect idea to spend some time together. It is not necessary to go out every time. Cuddling and movies sound like a sweet and comfortable date. It's easier for you to tire out of all the work of the day. A date might give you that energy boost that you need. No matter how long you have been dating, a date is perfect for you.

2. Share Your Day

Going through a hectic schedule is much work on themselves. When we come home to someone who will listen to us rant about every detail of our hectic day, our day gets better somehow. We get a weird sense of comfort to know that there might be someone willing to listen to us every day. The same goes the other way around; you need to listen attentively and remember the details. This shows that you care about your partner and your relationship turns sweeter.

3. Complement Each Other

When you try to look your best, put on your best dress and do on-point make-up. All you need is someone to compliment you on putting that charming smile on your face too. In a relationship, when both people compliment each other, not only does it sound sweet, but it boosts the confidence of the other partner. It would be best to remind your other half that they look perfect no matter how they dress or look because it's the love that matters.

4. Constant "I love You's"

When you randomly tell your partner how much you love them, nothing can be much sweeter than that. Those small moments of saying "I love you" can mean a lot to the other person. It might make their difficult day brighter. It can make them lose all their stress in an instant—elaborate your love. Tell them why you love them. Tell them you make them happy. It makes a relationship much more robust than before.

5. Physical Affection

Showing physical affection to each other sounds so romantic, as romantic as it feels. You were looking into each other's eyes, holding each other's hand and cuddling with each other. These small gestures may sound bland and ordinary. But they can feel like you have conquered the world. These are the feelings that make a bond more assertive and make a relationship sweeter. It would be best if you kept the flirting moving on to keep the spark alive in your relationship.

6. Gifts and Presents

You don't need a special occasion to gift your partner something. Surprise them randomly. It doesn't mean expensive gifts or unaffordable presents. Something sweet and personal will make them happy too. Like making their favorite dish or dessert, buying them their favorite perfume, or gift them something that personally means a lot to both of you. These simple ideas can make their whole day special.

Conclusion

Maintaining a relationship might not be as easy as it sounds, but when you are with the one you live and love to spend time with, then everything can be bearable. You need to keep the spark alive and keep each other strong individually as well.

Chapter 18:

7 Ways To Live Together In Harmony With Your Partner

A harmonious relationship can make a person's life happy and beautiful, but, unfortunately, not all of us are blessed with a harmonious relationship. It is essential to work on your relationship in order to make it work. Creating a harmonious bond between you and your partner can make your relationship healthier and more stable. The dream relationship of everybody is to feel loved, accepted, and respected but to achieve such a relationship, and you need to first work on yourself. You need to make sure that you are doing your best at making your partner feel loved.

Most people nowadays want to find their soulmates, but even when they see their soulmates, they don't have a peaceful relationship; the lack of harmony causes this.

Here are 7 ways to live together in harmony with your partner.

1. Accept Your Partners The Way They Are

The first step to a harmonious relationship is acceptance. It would be best to accept your partners the way they are; distancing them from yourself because of a simple mistake can lead to a toxic relationship. If you choose to love a person and be with them, you need to accept the good and bad in them. As they say that no one is perfect, we all are a work in progress. When you cannot receive your partner the way they are, a harmonious relationship cannot be achieved. It would help if you allowed them to evolve and support them throughout this journey.

2. Be Gentle and Compassionate

When you embody gentleness and compassion, your relationship bond deepens, and there is harmony in the relationship. Instead of jumping to conclusions and reacting dramatically, you need to respond with gentleness and understand your partner's feelings.

Compassion brings grace to a person. To achieve a harmonious relationship, you should give your partner grace to work on themselves, understand, and give them space to evolve and mature. It may take time, but it strengthens a relationship.

3. Expectations Should Be Released

With expectations comes disappointment. Expectations are the unspoken standards you expected your partner to live up to. When your partner does not live up to your expectations, you might feel upset or disappointed, but how can you have such high expectations from your partner about things that are unspoken. Work on letting go of these ideals that the society and your subconscious mind created about how a relationship should be. Release the attachment to situations turning out a specific way. Brace yourself for different outcomes of different situations. Don't expect too much from your partner because your partner, like you, cannot always live up to your expectation.

4. Personal Space in A Relationship

Every human being needs personal space; we often see couples that are always together. It may feel exciting and comforting at first, but everyone needs their personal space to think and function properly. After being with each other with no personal space, one can start feeling suffocated and may behave negatively. It would help if you had time to breathe, to expand, and to look within. To evolve, you need space. Personal space between couples proves that their relationship is healthy and robust.

5. Honesty

Honest communication is not just a factor to achieve a harmonious relationship but also to have any relationship at all. Not being truthful can cause conflicts and problems in a relationship. Moreover, being a liar can be a toxic trait that can cause your partner to end the relationship. But before being honest with your partner, you need to be honest with yourself. Know your true self, explore the good and bad in yourself. Don't hide your mistakes from your partner; instead, be honest and apologize to them before it is too late. Honesty is a crucial factor in achieving a harmonious relationship.

6. Shun Your Ego

Ego and harmony cannot simply go hand in hand; where ego exists, harmony cannot be established. Often by some people, ego is considered a toxic trait. This is the ego that stops a person from apologizing for his mistakes, which can create tension among the couple. The stubbornness to do things your way is caused by ego and can easily result in unwanted scenarios. These are not the components of a healthy relationship. So to establish a harmonious relationship, you should remove ego and learn to compromise a bit. By removing ego, you allow yourself to be more flexible and understanding.

7. Let Go if Unnecessary Emotional Pain

When you keep hurting over old resentments, you convert that pain into toxic feelings that are not good for a relationship. These poisonous feelings can make you make some bad decisions that may result in your partner feeling unsafe around you. This pain can cause you to bury your positives feeling inside. As a result of this, you may feel pessimistic and may exaggerate minor conflicts into something more. A person must let go of this emotional stress and pain. You can let go by going to a therapist or yoga and meditation. Once you have let go of the pain, your heart is now open to a peaceful and harmonious relationship.

To establish a harmonious relationship, you have to accept and understand your partner and work on yourself. Also, work on your radical integrity.

Chapter 19:

5 Ways To Make New Friends Without Leaving The House

With COVID-19 already hitting its second wave, we're getting more and more used to having to social distance (or distance socialize). But just because we may be stuck at home doesn't mean we can't make new friends. Here are some tips.

1. Reconnect with Old Friends

When people ask me how to make friends, my first suggestion is to reconnect with old friends. Why? Research finds that when we reconnect with past friends, we have a higher level of trust with them than we do current acquaintances. We start our friendship off with more shared memories and knowledge of one another, and so, our friendship potential is supercharged. Plus, most of us lose friends not because there were some insurmountable incompatibilities in the friendship, but because we got busy. Now's the time to reconnect with friends that you've fallen out of touch with who you wish you hadn't. This looks like: "Hey! It's been a while since we talked and I've been wondering how you are. What's new with you?" Take it from there, and if they're responsive, suggest a time to catch-up.

2. Connect Digitally

There are tons of ways to connect online. There are apps, like Bumble BFF, or Friender to meet people. Meetup.com has a variety of virtual events. You can join a Facebook group, post regularly, and ask if anyone is open to a virtual chat. People even connect with strangers through Instagram or Twitter. After commenting on someone's posts over time, eventually, start direct messaging them to develop a more meaningful connection. This looks like: "Hey! I've been such a fan of all the things you post. It seems like we have [insert thing] in common. I was wondering if you'd be open to connecting further over a virtual chat.

3. Turn Acquaintances Into Friends

We all have some people swirling in our lives who we'd love to get to know a bit better. It could be someone from your old book club or biking group or a friend of a friend you met at a gathering. You can turn these acquaintances into friends by taking the initiative to reach out and ask them to meet up one-on-one. This looks like: "Hey! It's been a while since we had a chance to connect. I've been meaning to reach out and see if you'd be open to hanging out sometime."

4. Become Friends with People You Already See Regularly

When we become friends with people we see regularly (like our neighbors or our co-workers), we capitalize on something called the mere exposure effect, which describes our tendency to like people the more familiar they are to us. One study involved planting strangers in a large lecture course for varying numbers of classes. At the end of the semester, students in the class were asked who they liked best amongst the strangers. It turns out they preferred the strangers who showed up for the most classes. This was true even though the students didn't remember any of the strangers AND didn't interact with any of them during the class. Because of the mere exposure effect, we already have some friendship traction when we try to build relationships with people we see regularly. This looks like: "Hey! I know we've been working together for a while and I've been meaning to find some time for us to get to know each other more. I was wondering if you wanted to set aside some time for a virtual coffee?"

5. Tell Friends or Family To Put You In Touch With Someone You Might Get Along With

When friends put us in touch with their friends, they pre-vet our connections. Research also finds that when we're friends with our friend's friends, we're less likely to be lonely. This may be because now, every time our friend and their friend spend time together, they'll consider inviting us to join. It's a win-win all around. This looks like: "Hey! I've been wanting to connect with some new people. Do you know anyone who you think I'd get along with who you'd be willing to connect me to?"

The common thread here is that if you want to make friends while you're stuck at home, you're going to have to take initiative. It'll pay off. One study found that the more people thought that making friends takes effort, the less lonely they were years later, and other research finds that the more we take initiative, the happier we are with our social circle. I know it can be scary to reach out, especially when we fear rejection, but according to the research, we overestimate our likelihood of being rejected. It's not as scary as it seems. It's easy to get lonely when you're stuck at home all day, but you don't have to be. Just reach out.

Chapter 20:

10 Thoughts That Can Destroy Relationships

You might enjoy the beauty and joy that comes with being in a loving and committed relationship, but it's not always butterflies and beds of roses. It's ubiquitous for you or your partner to transform your insecurities into fears and negative thoughts, but they don't treat you right; they may take a toll on your relationship. Negative thoughts may turn into negative actions, which can lead to unhealthy communication, and could impact how you start seeing your significant other. If you relate to any of the below thoughts, it might be time to re-evaluate your relationship and how you view the situation.

1. They Don't Love Me Anymore

Although it's pretty common to worry about whether the sparks of love are still alive in your partner's heart or not, constantly asking them whether they still love you might do more harm than good. It could stir up a lot of conflicts based on your insecurities and fears. Even if your partner reassures you by saying that they love you, it could put them in doubt as to there must be a matter causing these concerns. Instead of swinging and jumping to conclusions, communicate effectively with your partner in a way that's suitable for both of you.

2. The Power Word "Should"

It is more or less a major red flag to not tell your partner about what you're thinking rather than automatically assuming that they should know how to read your mind. Blaming your partner for understanding the things that are affecting you secretly, like, "he should know how much it bothers me when he doesn't give me time" or "she should understand how busy i am these days" isn't fair at all. You should be able to voice all your frustrations but in a way that you make your partner understand and not push them away.

3. The Blame Game

It's easier to point fingers at your partner and blame them for your spoiled mood rather than taking actions against yourself. Blaming them only postpones any improvements that are needed in your relationship. Instead, try talking to them about it. Tell them when they are wrong and apologize for something that you did to hurt them. We can never predict or control others' emotions, but we can very well hold our own.

4. Overactive Imagination

This mostly happens when you're overthinking about a situation and jump straight to conclusions without having any actual evidence. For instance, if your partner is coming home late at night and they're telling you it's because of the heavy workload, you automatically assume it's because they're having an affair and they're lying to you. These may happen when you have a piece of unattended emotional baggage from previous relationships. It's important to understand that you know your partner well, and they will never do such a thing to hurt you. Have a conversation with your partner about this and seek reassurance if needed.

5. Comparing and Contrasting

You start to put your partner under the pressure of unrealistic expectations when you compare them with a person you see as ideal. For example, if you met your best friend's boyfriend and witnessed an action they did, and you wished that your boyfriend should do the same, you might be disrespecting your partner by asking them to change into who they aren't. It's unhealthy to put that sort of pressure on them. Instead, ask your partner politely if they're willing to do that for you since you liked a particular quality or trait in a person, but you should also tell them that they are lovable regardless.

6. Fantasizing

Unless you are in a toxic relationship, reminiscing and fantasizing about someone other than your partner might badly affect your relationship. It's because you will keep thinking about the possibilities of being with someone else rather than working on the flaws of your relationship. This might destroy your relationship in ways you can't even imagine.

7. All or Nothing

Seeing your partner as a perfect human being without mistakes, flaws, or imperfections is an idea for destruction. Having extreme thoughts that they can do no wrong or thinking that they always do the wrong thing can mess up with your own and your partner's mental health. Try accepting their failures and mistakes, and keep in mind that, like you, they're just ordinary human beings.

8. Label Slinging

Constantly putting labels on your partner, like calling them lazy when they couldn't complete their chores or calling them insensitive if they don't address a particular issue, may cause problems in your relationship. Instead, we should try to see the positive things in them and help them improve themselves.

9. You Think You Can't Compete with Their Ex

Their ex is their ex for a reason. Constantly trying to be like them and asking about them isn't helpful in any way; it can make your relationship weak, and your partner frustrated.

10. You Think That You're Hard to Love

Worrying about pushing your partner away while addressing your insecurities is normal, but that doesn't in any way mean that you're hard to love. Everyone is special and unique in their tracks and can be loved by their partner no matter what.

Conclusion

While these thoughts might be the perfect recipe to destroy your relationship, a little effort, and hard work into it can go a long way and save your relationship.

Chapter 21:

9 Ways To Tell If They're Really Into You

When you like someone, you often want that person to like you back, but even if you feel like they like you, you are unsure. Sometimes, the other person is just being a bit friendly, but we think that maybe they are interested in us, which can cause some awkward situations. So the best way to avoid these awkward situations is to confirm that they like you before you make a move. Usually, when someone wants someone, their actions speak the truth. It could be the way they look at you, the way they talk to you, or any other activity. Here are nine ways to tell if someone is interested in you or are they just being nice.

1. They Maintain Eye Contact with Your While They Talk

When you are talking to that person and maintain eye contact with you, it means that they care about you because they listen to what you care about. It shows that they are paying attention and listening to you, and this mostly means that the person sitting in front of you is genuinely interested in you.

2. They Will Share More About Themselves

When someone likes you, they will like you to know more about them. They will want to get closer to you and share things with you. When someone tells us something, they also want to know more about you. When someone does that, you feel it because when someone starts telling you things, they have become rather fond of you or, in other words, like you.

3. They Want To Know More

We all want to know more about the person we like, but sometimes we are too shy, but everyone is different, and not everyone feels shy about letting you know that they want to know more about you. So if someone asks you a question about you, then don't hesitate to answer because now you know that they are definitely into you, and sometimes the other person just doesn't want to end the conversation, so they start asking a ton of questions.

4. They Tease You

As childish as it may sound, haven't we all been friendly with our crushes and joked around with them, just to let them know that we like them. If you like someone, you would want them to think that you are an entertaining person. So, if someone is teasing you and joking around you, it could be a sign that they like you.

5. They Lightly Touch You

When someone likes you, they would likely touch you lightly, not in a wrong way but rather in a sweet, subtle way. For example, if someone puts your hair behind your ear or grazes your leg with their "accidentally." This means that they want to be close to you because they feel interested in you.

6. They Usually Point Their Feet Towards You

Psychology says when someone's interested in you, they usually point their feet towards you while you are talking, and even when they are talking to someone else but still point their feet towards you, it means that they like you. Although, you may not understand why it's just human nature.

7. They Try To Find a Place Next To You

Although they say that when you genuinely like someone, distance doesn't matter. Who wouldn't want to be with someone they like, and if someone likes you, they will want to stay next to you. Take standing in a line for something as an example. If someone likes you, they would want to stand right next to you and avoid any distance from you at all.

8. They Often What To Meet With You

If someone likes you, they would want to see you as often as they can. Sometimes they would ask for your phone number through excuses, and sometimes they would suddenly make plans so that they could see you again.

9. Your Opinion Matters To Them

When making an important decision, they want to know what you think about it and put your opinion in their list of priorities. This shows that they are really into you.

Conclusion

It is not hard to figure out if someone's into you or not. You need to pay close attention to the tiniest of things.

Chapter 22:

6 Behaviors That Keep You Single

Dating may not be as easy as it is shown in all those romantic Hollywood movies. There is so much more than appearance and stability in dating someone. And when you are old enough to be involved with someone, you sometimes find yourself uninterested. You think about how everyone your age has already started dating while you are back there eating junk and watching Netflix. It might appear to you that being in a relationship is tiresome, and you stop trying for it. Everyone has a different preference when it comes to finding someone for themselves. You tend to look for someone that matches your knight in the shining armor, which makes it hard for you to find someone you need.

Be true to you yourself while finding someone to date. Looking for someone with the expectation that you are rich and handsome would be foolish. It would be best if you worked on yourself more than that. Make yourself ease around with people but no so much that they start to get annoyed. Don't get in your way.

1. Trust Is Essential

Trusting each other is an important factor for dating someone. If you don't trust your partner even in the slightest, then nothing will matter. You will constantly doubt each other. Both of you will eventually fall apart if there is no trust. And if you have trust issues, it will be difficult for you to find someone worthy. But, if you trust too quickly, then it's only natural that you will break your bubble of expectations. Be friendly. Try to get to know them properly before making any assumptions about them. You don't want to go around hesitating about everything. Find yourself a reliable partner that trusts you too.

2. Too Many Expectations

Expecting too much from your partner will lead to only one thing. It leads towards Disappointment. It would help if you let them be. Don't expect things to go your way always. Your knight in the shining armour may be a bookworm because people find love in the most unexpected places. It doesn't always mean to keep no expectations at all. To keep the expectations low. You will get surprised constantly when you don't know what's coming your way. Don't let people cloud your judgment and keep high standards about a relationship. Everyone has their share of ups and downs. Comparison with others will not be suitable for your relationship.

3. Have Self-Confidence

One has to respect itself before anything else can. You have to have self-esteem in you for people to take you seriously. It is true "you can't love someone unless you learn to love yourself first." You tend to feel insecure about yourself. Everything around you seems too perfect for you. And you constantly think that your partner will stop loving you one day. That fear of yours will get you nowhere. Try to give yourself as much care you can. It doesn't hurt to be loved.

4. Don't Overthink

You found a guy, and He seems to be excellent. But you start to overthink it. Eventually, you let go. That is what you shouldn't have done. Just try to go with the flow sometimes. Don't try too hard for it. Go for it the easy way. Overthinking will lead you to make up scenarios that never happened. Just let it be and see where it goes. Be easy so people can approach you. Think, don't overthink.

5. Involving Too Many People

When you initially start dating, you get nervous. People get help from their friends sometimes. But it is not necessary to get every move through them. Involving them in everything will only get your partner get uncomfortable and get you frustrated. People tend to give a lot of opinions of their own. You will get confused. So, it is good to keep these things to yourself. Be mindful in giving them a brief report from time to time. However, keep them at a reasonable distance.

6. Giving Up Too Quickly

If it doesn't work initially, it does not mean that it will never work. Patience is an essential element when it comes to dating anyone. Don't give up too quickly. Try to make it work until it's clear that it won't. Give it your all. Compromise on things you can. Because if both of you are not willing to compromise, it will not work between you both. It will work out in the end if it's meant to be. Don't push it if it's not working too.

Conclusion

It is hard; it keeps going at a pace. But all you must need is that spark that keeps it alive. Make it work until it doesn't. Go for it all. Make commitments only when you are sure about your choice. And be true to your words. Who wants to be single forever?

Chapter 23:

6 Ways To Be More Confident In Bed

Confidence is something a lot of people inherit naturally, while others could work on. When you're confident and comfortable in your skin, people assume that you have a reason to be, and then they react and respect you accordingly. You can be confident all you want at work or on dates, but what about being confident in bed? Being confident sexually can be enjoyable for both you and your partner. It isn't just at ease sexual, but also it's comfortable with the way you express and experience your sexuality.

Sexual confidence can be measured by how authentically you can relate intimately either with yourself or your partner and how pure and vulnerable you are in that sexual space where you feel like giving your 100 percent to be yourself and communicate the pleasure you desire. Building your confidence in bed can crucially improve your sex life. Here are some tips on how to be more confident in bed.

1. Do What You're Already Confident In

Even if you are insecure and think you lack sexual skills, there must be at least a tiny thing that you might be good at. Maybe you don't feel confident enough about your kissing skills, but you're a great cuddler, or perhaps you feel shaky about touching and teasing but are good vocally. Focus on what you're good at and polish that skill every time you're in bed with your partner. This will help you boost your confidence and might even convince you to try something new with them.

2. Try Something New

Once you start considering yourself as the master of that one skill you have been practicing, you would end up craving to try new things. Start with the things you're less comfortable with; maybe stepping out of your comfort zone might be enjoyable for you after all. You neither have to perfect the skill nor be a master of it, just trying it out can be fun in itself. It might be helpful to broaden the sexual script so that it doesn't look the same every time and bore your partner, but instead, trying new things can be an excellent adventure for you as well as your partner.

3. Laugh It Off If You Trip Up

You can't be good at everything you try in bed, nor should you be. What matters is how well you keep your attitude, and if you can have fun with it and have a great laugh if things go south, that's an achievement in itself. If you have already built-up consistent self-confidence, then you can laugh it out loud on something that you can't get a grip on. After all, there might always be some things you'll be bad at and others in which you'll be a master.

4. Focus on What You Love About Your Body

There are instances where we will be utterly insecure about our bodies and features. There are some physical traits that we don't like but have made peace with, while others that we want but don't appreciate enough. The next time you look in the mirror, focus more on what you like about your face and body, be confident in them, and the things you don't like about yourself will vanish automatically.

5. Wear What Makes You Feel Confident

There is no particular stuff you have to wear or the way you have to look to feel more confident, but if you wear a look that you think looks great, you must go with it. Chances are, you will start feeling better about yourself instantly. If you feel more confident wearing lipstick, then wear it to bed, or if you think sexier wearing a lotion, use it before bed. Do whatever makes you feel like a total hottie.

6. Repeat A Mantra

We have all heard of the phrase "fake it till you make it." So, there's no harm in faking affirmations till you start believing in them. Keep repeating "I'm confident, I've got this" till it gets through. Affirmations increase how positively we feel about ourselves.

Conclusion

The task of becoming confident may seem daunting, but these small sub-tasks are an easy way to start. Another plus point is once you have practiced these techniques in bed, the confidence will spill over into every area of your life.

Chapter 24:

6 Relationship Goals To Have

We live in a generation where the term "relationship goals" has become a part of the trendy vernacular. It may seem more like a hashtag than anything else, but we all are eager to go into the depth of its meaning. A beautiful photo of a stunning couple having a good time together. Relationship goals. A cute text message sent to a girlfriend from his boyfriend. Relationship goals. A perfect wedding? Relationship goals. All these might seem sweet and enviable and look like an absolute dream, and it doesn't mean that these come off as accessible to them. If you have ever been in a relationship, you would know exactly what I'm saying.

Love is not always fireworks, passion, and butterflies. Relationships are not just date nights, kisses, and cuddles. And love is not that glamorous as it looks on social media. But when you strive to build something together, involving your selflessness, commitment, and even sweat and tears, those are actual relationship goals. Here is a list of what relationship goals you must have with your partner.

1. Always Do New Things Together

Sure, alone time might be great, but together time is where the magic happens too. Avoiding your relationship becoming mundane and a rut, you both should try to do new things together. This could be choosing any vacation spot or having an exciting adventure together. You both should make a list of all the things you want to do with each other and keep adding stuff that might pop later. Tick things off as you go, and you'll never run out of things to do together.

2. Be Each Other's Biggest Supporters

Perhaps one of the best things about being in a relationship is that you'll always have someone in your corner. Regardless of how crazy or unrealistic your dreams and goals may sound, your partner should be your biggest supporter. Seeing the person, you love believing in could come off as a massive motivation to achieve your goals. This goes both ways; both men and women need to feel emotionally supported. You both should take some time out to discuss what emotional support looks like to you, what and when you need it, and then provide the said support for each other.

3. Put Each Other First

Putting each other first in your relationship will ensure that you're paying attention to each other's needs and making sure they are being met. You have become selfless with each other, and you both strive to make each other happy and would do anything to put a smile on each other's faces. You complement each other, protect each other, support and love each other, no matter the obstacles or circumstances.

4. Know The Importance of Alone Time

As much as you don't want to keep your hands off your partner in the early stages of your relationship, it's essential to know that you both need time alone to recharge and refill your cup. Spending all of your time together isn't sustainable, and alone time is significant. It will help you maintain your individuality, allow you breathing space, and encourage a closer relationship with each other when you spend time together.

5. Keep The Physical Connection Going

Sex isn't always an option when dealing with different phases of your relationship. There are going to be times when it might not be physically or mentally possible. But this in no way means that you should stop all physical connections. Physically touching the person you love releases an oxytocin hormone; this feel-good love hormone reduces stress and makes you feel wonderful things. You can stay physically connected by holding hands, cuddling, or simply leaning on one another.

6. Speak Positively About Each Other

Speaking ill of your partner with others is not only disrespectful to them, but it's also disrespectful to your relationship. Sure, you can vent in tough times, but make sure you talk about the actions and behaviors that upset you and not their personality traits. Always speak positively and kindly of each other. Even if their behavior irritates you, focus more on the characteristics you love of them and let it pass.

Conclusion

Relationships are complicated but beautiful at the same time. As simple as the above factors may sound to you, these things take a lot of effort and hard work to be implemented. But when you do all of these with the person you love the most in the world, then all of it can be worth it.

Chapter 25:

9 Tips on How To Have A Strong Relationship

Who doesn't want a strong relationship? Everyone wants to have that high-level understanding with their partner that lasts a lifetime. It is scientifically proven that people who are in healthy relationships have less stress and more happiness.

Healthy relationship not only helps us increase our overall feelings of happiness, but stress-reduction also helps us improve our overall quality of physical and mental health that make every-day life more pleasing to go through. Relationships can be in the form of family, work, friendships, and also romantic ones. Depending on the area that matters the most to you at this very point in your life, you can choose to focus on that specific one until you feel you are ready to focus on the next.

If building powerful relationships is a priority of yours as it is mine, then stay with me till the end of this video because we will be discussing **9 Magical** Tips on How To Have A Strong Relationship with whoever you want. Let's Begin.

1. Listen to Each Other

This is the first and probably the most important thing that you might want to take note of. Just think, how many arguments have you had that went in the wrong direction just because no one was willing to simply just listen? In order to understand each other's point of view both parties must be willing to open up their ears instead of their mouths first. You need to have the stamina to listen to their side of the story before airing yours.

If you truly want a healthy relationship, then the foundations starts with a good listening ear. To listen not only when the other party have problems in their lives, but also when they have a problem with you. Develop a good sense of compassion and empathy in the process.

Bitter thoughts, grudge-holding, and negativity toward the other person only serve to weaken your relationships, not strengthen them. So try to understand each other, let the other person speak, and then sort things out in the best possible way.

2. Give Time For The Relationship To Grow

For any relationship to truly blossom, it is important to spend the necessary quality time together. Whether the relationship is with family members, friends, or lovers, it takes energy and effort nonetheless. Any amount of energy you spend on that person will reap its benefits later.

Now, I am not saying to drastically change your life or to go on adventures or expensive dates to make your relationship healthy. All you have to do is simply get yourself free for a day or night once a week and do something different together, like having a date night, playing games, cooking and eating, watching movies or whatever you like, just give your best at that time. Be present with them and don't be distracted checking your phone or replying work messages.

3. Give Time To Yourself

Now I needed to talk about this one right after the number two. I think a good relationship should be balanced. In the previous point, I talked about spending quality time in relationships, but I also don't mean that you should give all your energy to them or stop doing things that energizes your soul. Don't sacrifice your own hobbies for the sake of others. I agree that you need to take more initiative in relationships but at the same time you need to take care of your own happiness too. So give time to yourself and spend it doing things that fills your soul with happiness and gratefulness. You will feel recharged and fresh as a result when you engage in your relationships.

4. Learn To Appreciate Little Things

This point will touch more on the romantic relationship side of things. If you are in a relationship for quite a while, then there is a chance that you might get complacent and too comfortable. You might also gradually forget the little things that make the person special. As a result, the other person could potentially feel like you may be taking them for granted. To avoid this, you need to start making it a constant reminder to yourself to appreciate the little things your partner does for you. Say "I love you" to them, give cute little gifts, give them surprises and tell them how much they mean to you. You need to show your partner how much you love them so they never feel taken for granted. So yeah, start doing all this and make your bond strong!!

5. Learn To Forgive

It is well said, "relationships require a lot of forgiveness". As I mentioned earlier, bitter thoughts and grudge-holding just hurt your relationship in the long run. So, if you want a happy relationship then you should learn to forgive. If there is something on your mind that your partner did and you can't forget then sit and talk to them about it and try to come up with a good solution. If any of you makes any mistake, you should forgive them with a smiling face and tell them that these little mistakes can't lessen your love. Work on yourself, make your heart ready for what you see coming and even what you don't see coming, and let things go in the right direction. You need to make your heart learn to forgive, this is the only key.

6. Don't Expect Your Partner To Complete You

You should be confident about whatever you have. If you are looking for a healthy relationship, then you should not expect your partner to complete you. Sometimes, we expect things from our partners which we lack, and it can put a strain on your relationship. What you could do instead is to constantly work on yourself to the point that you feel you truly and rightfully deserving of every good thing that comes your way. That you feel secure and independent at the same time in the relationship. Loving yourself first goes a long way in maintaining a strong and healthy relationship with others.

7. Ways Of Showing Love

Different people show and receive love in their own unique ways. Understanding how the other party expresses or receives love is the key to building a strong relationship. Some people do it by caring for you while others express it through physical affection like hugs and kisses. If you don't know that the specific love language is between you and the other party then it might cause problems in the long run. To really ensure the other party feels loved you have to express it in the way that they receive the most strongly. Go find out what they are by asking them and then start giving it right away!

8. Be Flexible

If you want a healthy relationship, then you have to learn to be flexible as well. Flexible in the face of any changes that might occur in your relationship. It is a known fact that change is the only constant in life. We may never be prepared but we should do our best to adapt to new situations that we may find ourselves in. It is also therefore unrealistic not to expect our relationships to change as time progresses as well. Learn to adapt and grow in this new stage and you will be all the happier for it.

9. Make Decisions Jointly

A good and healthy relationship requires listening to each other's desires and concerns. While you may not always love to do the things that the other party wants, you should always try to find a compromise that suits both of your needs. Instead of insisting and making decisions all the time, try making decisions together that both of you will find enjoyable. Be it where to hang out, what to eat for a meal, where to go on a trip together, or even what kinds of products to buy for your home, make sure that the other party's points of view is heard so that they don't end up resenting you over the long run.

Chapter 26:

8 Signs Someone Misses You

Missing someone can be very painful, almost as if there is something incomplete about your life. You think about them all the time, and the more you try not to think of them, the more you end up doing that. You might find your thoughts wandering and can't seem to focus on anything other than them. You may either find comfort in binge eating or constantly go through their stuff. Well, you're not the only one who might be going through this torture. What if someone is experiencing the same stuff but for you? Here are some signs that tell you someone is missing you.

1. They Keep Track of Your Social Media

If they haven't unfriended, unfollowed, or blocked you yet, the chances are that they are still keeping track of you. If you find them constantly reacting to your stories or liking your pictures the minute you put them up, then they're visiting your profile again and again. They have kept their slot open for making a conversation or giving you a hint to try to make conversation with them.

2. Did They Find Your Replacement Yet?

For someone ready to move on, it takes a second to find a replacement. If they haven't found one yet, the chances are that they are still reminiscing over you. They're hoping that you'll reconnect and thus, still pine after you. Even if they're hooking up with someone as a rebound, chances are they're doing everything in their power to forget you but are failing miserably.

3. They Reach Out To You Randomly

Receiving those drunk late-night texts/calls? They're miserable, and all they want to do is talk to you. If they were out there having the time of their life, they wouldn't even remember you let alone bother to text or call you. If they do, it's obviously because you're on their mind and alcohol just gave them a head start to get in touch with you again.

4. Rousing Your Jealousy So You Would Notice Them

Have they suddenly started posting a lot about their new life on social media? Chances are they're most certainly trying hard to make you sit up and take notice of them. If they're hanging out with a lot of people that you've never seen or heard of and having a fantastic time, then they're trying to make you jealous.

5. They Throw Shade at You

If they're making snide comments or remarks about you or a new partner, they're still clearly hurt and miss you. They might pass a statement on your outfit or your appearance and lash out at you, trying to make you feel as bad as they do. They may also show disapproval of your new date and point out negative things about them. It's clear that they still haven't moved on and clung to that thin thread of hope.

6. They Do Things to Get Your Attention

Do they post stuff that points towards you? Or do they write cute love letters or poems mentioning you? This is a pretty obvious sign that they miss you and want to get back in their life. They might also ask your friends about you and crash those uninvited parties because they want to see you. You might also see them around more than usual.

7. They Hoard Your Stuff

Are they still keeping your shirt/hoodie and making excuses not to give it even when you have asked them a million times? Or are they keeping even the most useless thing that you might have given them years ago? It's probably because they go through this stuff and relive all the old memories associated with them. They're still not ready to give them up and move on.

8. From The Horse's Mouth

The most obvious and straightforward sign that someone misses you? They tell you themself! Some people don't like to play games and do unnecessary things to gain your attention or throw hints and clues at you and wait for you to notice them. They tell you straight away that they miss you and they want to do something about it.

Conclusion

Now that you have all the signs on your plate, it's up to you whether you want to give them a second chance or move on from all of this. The choice is yours!

Chapter 27:

6 Signs You Are Emotionally Unavailable

In times of need, all we want is emotional comfort. The people around us mainly provide it. But the question is, will we support them if the need arises? You might be emotionally unavailable for them when they need you. It is necessary to have some emotional stability to form some strong bonds. If you are emotionally unapproachable, you will have fewer friends than someone you stand mentally tall. It is not harmful to be emotionally unavailable, but you need to change that in the long run. And for that, you need to reflect on yourself first.

It would help if you always were your top priority. While knowing why you are emotionally unapproachable, you need to focus on yourself calmly. Giving respect and talking is not enough for someone to rely on you. You need to support them whenever needed. Talk your mind with them. Be honest with them. But not in a rude way, in a comforting way. So, next time they will come to you for emotional support and comfort. If you are relating to all these things, then here are some signs that confirm it.

1. You Keep People At A Distance

It is usual for an emotionally unavailable person to be seen alone at times. They tend to stay aloof at times; that way, they don't have to be emotionally available. And even if you meet people, you always find it challenging to make a bond with them. You might have a few friends and family members close to you. But you always find meeting new people an emotionally draining activity. You also might like to hang out with people, but opening up is not your forte. If you are emotionally unavailable, then you keep people at a hands distance from you.

2. You Have Insecurities

If you struggle to love yourself, then count it as a sign of emotional stress. People are likely to be unavailable emotionally for others when they are emotionally unavailable for themselves too. We always doubt the people who love us. How can they when I, myself, can't? And this self-hatred eventually results in a distant relationship with your fellow beings. Pampering yourself time by time is essential for every single one of us. It teaches us how one should be taken care of and how to support each other.

3. You Have A Terrible Past Experience

This could be one of the reasons for your unapproachable nature towards people. When you keep some terrible memory or trauma stored inside of you, it's most likely you cannot comfort some other being. It won't seem like something you would do. Because you keep this emotional difference, you become distant and are forced to live with those memories, making things worse. It would help if you talked things out. Either your parents or your friends. Tell them whatever is on your mind, and you will feel light at heart. Nothing can change the past once it's gone, but we can work on the future.

4. You Got Heartbroken

In most cases, people are not born with this nature to be emotionally unavailable. It often comes with heartbreak. If you had a breakup with your partner, that could affect your emotional life significantly. And if it was a long-term relationship, then you got emotionally deprived. But on the plus side, you got single again. Ready to choose from scratch. Instead, you look towards all the negative points of this breakup. Who knows, maybe you'll find someone better.

5. You Are An Introvert

Do you hate going to parties or gatherings? Does meeting with friends sound tiresome? If yes, then surprise, you are an introvert. Social life can be a mess sometimes. Sometimes we prefer a book to a person. That trait of ours makes us emotionally unavailable for others. It is not a bad thing to stay at home on a Friday night, but going out once in a while may be healthy for you. And the easiest way to do that is to make an extrovert friend. Then you won't need to make an effort. Everything will go smoothly.

6. You Hate Asking For Help

Do you feel so independent that you hate asking for help from others? Sometimes when we get support from others, we feel like they did a favor for us. So, instead of asking for help, we prefer to do everything alone, by ourselves. Asking for aid, from superior or inferior, is no big deal. Everyone needs help sometimes.

Conclusion

Being emotionally unavailable doesn't make you a wrong person, but being there for others gives us self-comfort too. It's not all bad to interact with others; instead, it's pretty fun if you try. It will make your life much easier, and you will have a lot of support too.

Chapter 28:

7 Ways To Make Your Marriage Sweeter

At the beginning of a marriage, one can feel the excitement and sparks that come from its newness. For example, the butterflies you feel before going on a honeymoon can make you feel surprisingly on top of the world. It is the start of a marriage that makes you feel this way. Everything feels fresh at the beginning of marriage as your partner surprises you and makes you feel special.

But as time goes on, the marriage becomes boring. This can often lead to an end of a marriage if not enough effort is put in; to prevent this, you could always keep your wedding fresh and exciting. Even though now both of you are not the same person you used to be in each other's eyes, you could still maintain that tingly sensation by trying to be more surprising. Here are seven ways to keep your marriage sweeter.

1. Keep Surprising Each Other

At the start of every marriage, partners often surprise each other with flowers, gifts, or a surprise date. These surprises cause the other partner to feel beloved. Still, people usually stop shaking their partners with such things as time goes on. By continuing to surprise your partner with gifts, flowers, and sweet notes, you keep your marriage fresh. After a while, you learn about the likes and dislikes of your partner. You can easily use that to your advantage by buying them flowers they like or small presents that make them happy. The happiness caused by these small gestures of love can keep the relationship from becoming dull. So don't let the element of surprise die.

2. Ask Them Out On A Date

A relationship often begins with a date, and the date makes you feel nervous and excited. Meeting your partner for the first few times can make you want to look the best version of yourself and continue your efforts to look and be the best for your partners. So don't stop the actions. Ask your partner out on a fancy date to make them happy. Even if you are ordering food from outside, you could still light up some candles and set the table with a fancy dinner set. This could make your partner feel special, and the freshness of the marriage doesn't die with time.

3. Try Something New Together

Always try to do something new, like watching movies you liked as a teenager or eating something you haven't tried before; it awakens the excitement your partner feels throughout the day. Try going ice skating or skateboarding together as a fun activity, taking time from your adult routine, and going hiking and other activities to have fun together.

4. Speak About Your Feelings Towards Them

Try voicing your thoughts about them. Don't shy away from words and tell them regularly how much they mean to you or how strongly you feel towards them; simple sentences like "i love you" can profoundly affect your partner. Please don't take your partner for granted but make them feel good about themselves and tell them how important they are in your life. This can make them appreciate your presence, and the relationship will remain fresh.

5. Set Life Goals Together

You and your partner can decide on some goals that you can achieve together as a couple. It can be any goal, as a financial goal, or exploring the world together. You could save money for vacations together. During this journey, you can motivate each other but can still have fun. Moreover, when you work as a team, it will also strengthen your bond.

6. Turn Off Your Phone

When spending time with each other, try turning off your phone. This will show your partner how important they are to you. Focus on their words and respond actively. Studies show that a relationship can end when you focus more on social media apps than on your partner. Using too many social media apps can distance you from your partner; try spending more time with them than using your mobile phone to re-establish your bond.

7. Greet Each Other With Excitement

When a relationship begins, we often see couples embracing each other with love and passion even when they met just yesterday. Still, as time passes, couples can be seen greeting each other with just a simple hello or a short hug. Greeting your partner with excitement and enthusiasm can make them long to meet you. They would be excited all day long because of the way you greet them. This can ensure that the excitement of the relationship doesn't die. You can greet them with a warm, comforting hug or simply a few exciting words; saying mushy things can also make them feel loved, like "i missed you" when they come back home from work.

Conclusion

By following the above ways, you can keep your partner happy and your marriage fresh and exciting.

Chapter 29:

10 Ways To Attract Love

The following ideas are to attract true love and romance into your life. These fun and practical little tips will magnify your energy and get the Law of Attraction sending more love your way whether you're single or need a little spark in your relationship

1. Get Specific: What Kind Of A Relationship Would You Like In Your Life?

Take out a piece of paper or open up a document on your computer and list out what kind of relationship you would like to have in your life. What does it look like? How does it work? Will you get married? Get specific. God/The Universe/Source Energy is always in the details.

2. Let Go of Your Past, De-Clutter And Move Forward

This means not talking about 'him or her' as much and perhaps getting rid of old love letters or emails that keep you stuck in the past. It's time to pave the way for a new person to step forward. They can't arrive when you're still pining over someone else.

3. Watch Movies Of The Love You Would Like To Attract

Without a doubt 'The Notebook' is the romantic movie that most people refer to when they think of the type of love they would like to attract. Go to IMDB and search for romantic movies and create a 'must watch list'.

4. Show Yourself The Love You Think You Deserve

It's really important to know how good (or not so good) your levels of self-esteem are. You really need to love yourself in order to attract a relationship that is sustainable. The truth? Otherwise, you'll be attracting someone that will want to fix you or will magnify your need to take care of yourself better. This can be a good thing, but unless you shine light on the need for self-love and self-care then it can turn ugly very fast. So, this is why it's so important to treat yourself well and show yourself the love you think you deserve.

How will you love yourself today? Ask yourself this powerful question at least 3 times per day.

5. Buy Yourself Flowers Or Tickets To Something You Want To Watch

Surrounding yourself with bunches of fresh and beautiful blooms is a great way to raise your vibration. It encapsulates the essence of springtime and is really lovely and feminine. Also take yourself on a date to the movies. Watch something that you really want to see. This is an act of strengthening levels of self love.

6. Create Space In Your Bedroom For Your Lover

I learnt this one from 'The Game of Life and How to Play It' where Florence Scovel Shinn writes about the importance of demonstrating something called 'active faith'. It's where you create space for whatever it is that you wish to welcome in your life. By creating space in your bedroom for your lover you are letting the Universe know that you're ready. You can do this by just sleeping on one side of the bed, making drawer space available for his or her clothes.

7. Soul Mate Journal Exercise

Write a clear list of all of the things you would like to do with your soul mate. List out the dates, tourist attractions, events and fun things you can do together. Feel excited about sharing these experiences with someone.

8. Crystal Magic

Get some rose quartz to flow energy into and use it as an attraction point for manifesting love. Carry it with you as a reminder of the lover that is on track to find you soon.

9. Buy A Special Dinner Plate For Your Lover Or A Coffee Cup

Imagine making a cup of tea or coffee for your lover each morning. By buying a special cup you can visualize the process of having him/her there with you. The Universe will respond to this action.

10. Feel Energized When You See Others In Love

Don't be one of those people that see public displays of affection or people blissfully in love and allow it to activate your crabby/skeptical mind. You can only attract success when you are genuinely happy for others and their success. Allow yourself to be energized by the love that others share and affirm to yourself that your time is on its way very soon.

Chapter 30:

10 Ways Men Fall In Love

Genuine and true Love is so rare that when you encounter it in any form, it's a beautiful thing to be utterly cherished in whatever form it takes. But how does one get this genuine and true Love? Almost every romantic movie, we have seen that a guy meets a girl and, sure enough, falls head over heels for her. But translating that into the real world can be quite a task. The science of attraction works wonders for us. Sometimes we are instantly drawn to some people. On the other hand, we couldn't care less for others. And quite a few times, things flow naturally in our direction, making it all feel surreal and causing butterflies.

A famous psychologist once said: "Love is about an expansion of the self whereby another person's interests, values, social network, and finances become part of your life just as you share your resources with them."

A human mind is, nonetheless, a very complex organ. It can either makes you feel like you're on top of the world with its positive attitude or under it with its negative one. And a male mind, perhaps, seems always like a mystery to us. But it's not such rocket science that we can't get our hands on it. If you're developing feelings for someone and need a bit of guidance to get the man of your dreams to notice you and care about you, then you've just come to the right place!

Here are some ways about what a man needs to fall in Love.

1. Always Be Yourself

Keeping a façade of fake personality and pretending to be someone you're not can be a huge turn-off for men. Instead let the guy know the real you. Let them see who you really are and what you really have to offer. You will not only gain respect from them, but you wouldn't have to keep hiding behind a mask. If you're pretending to be someone else, that only suggests that you're not comfortable with yourself. And many guys will realize this shortcoming and quickly become disinterested. You don't have to dumb down your intellect or put a damper on your exuberant personality. Men like women who are completely honest with them from the start. Who shows them their vulnerable side as well as their opinionated and intelligent one. You're in no need to pretend that your IQ isn't off the charts. Be your genuine, miserable, confident, and independent self always. That way, he will know exactly what he's getting into.

2. Make Him Feel Accepted and Appreciated

From a simple thank you text to calling him and asking him about his day, making small gestures for him, and complimenting and praising him, a man needs it all. Men don't always show it, but they are loved to be told that they look good, they're doing a good job, or how intellectual they are. Sometimes men are confused about where women may stand, and they want to see that he's being supported beyond any superficial matter. When men share glimpses of their inner self with you and put themselves in a vulnerable position, which men rarely do, this is when it's crucial to make him feel rest assured that he will be accepted and appreciated. If women make men feel lifted high and admired, then it's pure magic for them. His heart will make such a deep connection with you that it can only be amplified from thereon.

3. Listen! Don't Just Talk

You would see a lot of men complain that they are not heard enough. And quite frankly, it is true. It's essential to establish a mutual balance in the conversation. Women shouldn't make it all about themselves. They need to let the men speak and hear them attentively and respond accordingly. Ask him questions about his life and his passion, his likes, and dislikes. That way, he'll know that you are genuinely interested in him. Men have a lot to say when you show that you can listen. They'll be more inclined to say the things that matter.

4. Laugh Out Loud With Him

Men tend to make the women of their liking laugh a lot. When you're laughing, you're setting off chemicals in a guy's brain to feel good. Make him feel like he has a great sense of humor, and he's making you happy with his silly and jolly mannerism. Similarly, men are attracted to women who have a spirit that can make them feel good. Tell him enjoyable stories, roast people with him, jump in on his jokes and laugh wholeheartedly with him. He will become attracted to you.

5. Look Your Best

You don't have to shred a few pounds, or get clear, glowing skin, or change your hairstyle to impress the men of your liking. You have to be confident enough in your skin! Men love a confident woman who feels secure about herself and her appearance. You don't even have to wear body-hugging clothes or tight jeans to make him drool over you (Of course, you can wear them if you want). But a simple pair of jeans and a t-shirt can go a long way too. Just remember to clean yourself up nice, put on nice simple clothes, wear that unique perfume, style up your hair a bit, and voila! You're good to go.

6. Be Trustworthy

Another reason that men instantly attract you is when they have the surety that they can trust you with anything and everything. According to love and marriage experts "Trust is not something all loving relationships start with, but successful marriages and relationships thrive on it. Trust is so pervasive that it becomes part of the fabric of these strong relationship." If you want to win a man's heart, reassure him that he can be vulnerable around you and make him feel accepted and secure.

7. Don't Try to Change Him

"He's completely right for me... if only he didn't dress up like that or snore during his sleep."
Sure, we might have a few things on our list about how our partner should be, but that doesn't mean we should forcibly try to change their habits. He might have a few annoying habits that will get on your nerves now and then, but that shouldn't be a dealbreaker for you. Instead, we should accept him with all his wits and flaws. You shouldn't just tolerate his little quirks but rather try to admire them too. If something about him is bothering you, try talking to him politely about it. And he might consider changing it for you!

8. Have Intellectual Conversations with Him

There's nothing that a man finds sexier than women with opinion and intellect. Get his views on a news article, engage him in a heated debate about controversial topics, put your views out the front; even if they clash with his, especially if they conflict with his, he'd be more interested and intrigued about knowing your stance. Show your future partner that you can carry on an intelligent conversation with him anytime he likes.

9. Be Patient

I can't stress enough that patience is perhaps the most vital key to getting a guy to fall for you. It would be best if you gave him time to analyze and process his feelings for you. If you tend to rush him on the subject, you might end up disappointed. Even if you do lose your cool, don't let him know it. Just be patient and consistent, and don't come off as too clingy or needy. If you appear too desperate, it's going to turn him off of the relationship entirely.

10. Let Him Know You're Thinking of Him

In the early days of dating, you might be hesitant to tell him that you're thinking of him. You love it when he texts you randomly, saying he's thinking about you, so why not reciprocate it? Invest your time, energy, and efforts in him. Leave him short, sweet notes, or text him in the middle of the day saying that he is on your mind or sending him a greeting card with a cute personal message. Don't overdo it by reminding him constantly if he does not respond. None of these screams' overboard' and are guaranteed to make him smile.

Conclusion

I hope this article deconstructed and gave you some insights into what makes a man fall for a woman. As the saying goes, 'Men are from mars and women are from Venus and Venus is great, but surely, we need to know about the inner workings of mars too.' Just keep the above tips in mind, be consistent and commit to him considerably, and you're good to go! If you found this video helpful, don't forget to like, subscribe, comment, and share this with someone important to you. I hope you learned something valuable today. Take care, have a good rest, and till the next video ☺

Chapter 31:

6 Signs Your Love Is One Sided

While some things are better one-sided, like your favorite ice-cream cone that you don't want to share, your high school diary that knows all your enemies and crushes, and a game of solitaire. But a healthy relationship? Now that should be a two-sided situation. Unfortunately, when you're stuck in a one-sided relationship, it becomes easy to fool yourself every day that what you are experiencing is normal, when in reality, it could actually be toxic or even unworthy and loveless.

They could physically be sitting next to you, but you will find yourself being alone because of your emotional needs not being taken care of. Even though you have committed yourself to your partner, there's a fundamental difference between being selfless in love and giving it all without receiving anything at all. It might be possible that you're in denial, but the below signs of your one-sided love are hard to ignore.

1. You're Constantly Second-Guessing Yourself

If you don't get enough reassurance from your partner and constantly wonder if you are pretty enough, or intelligent enough, or funny enough, and always trying to live up to your partner's expectations, then you're definitely in a one-sided relationship. You tend to focus all of your energy and attention on being liked instead of being your true self and nurtured by your partner. It would be best if you always were your authentic self so the people who genuinely deserve you can get attracted to you and get relationships that match the true you.

2. You Apologize More Than Needed

Everyone makes mistakes. We are not some divine creatures who are all perfect and have no flaws. Sometimes you're at fault, sometimes your partner is. But if you end up saying sorry every single time, even if you had no idea about the fight, then maybe take a deeper look at your relationship. You may think that you're saving your relationship by doing this, but trust me, this is a very unhealthy sign. Cori Dixon-Fyle, founder and psychotherapist at Thriving Path, says, "Avoiding conflict results in dismissing your feelings." Solving fights should always be a team approach and not just one person's responsibility.

3. You're Always Making Excuses For Your Partner

Playing defence is excellent, but only on a soccer team. Suppose you are doing it constantly for your partner and justifying their behaviors to your circle of friends, family, and work colleagues. In that case, you're overlooking something that they are most likely seeing. If the people in your life are constantly alarming you, then maybe you should focus on your partner and see where the signs are coming from.

4. You Feel Insecure About Your Relationship

If you are never indeed at ease with your partner and often question the status of your relationship, then it's a clear sign that you are in a one-sided relationship. If you focus more on analyzing yourself, becoming more alluring, and choosing words or outfits that will keep your partner desiring you, then it's a major red flag. To feel unsettled and all-consumed in a relationship is not only exhausting, but it's also sustainable. Feeling constantly depleted in your relationship is also a sign that it's one-sided.

5. You're Giving Too Much

Giving too much and expecting just a little can never work in the long run. Suppose you're the only one in the relationship who makes all the plans. Do all the chores, remember all the important dates and events, consider stopping or making your partner realize that they aren't giving much in the relationship. Often when people give, they have some expectations in the back of their mind that the giving will be returned, but things fall apart when the other person never had those intentions. It's normal for a short while for one partner to carry the load more than the other; all relationships go through such stages, but constantly engaging in it is unhealthy.

6. You're Never Sure About How They Are Feeling

You can't read people's minds, nor are the communications transparent; you may end up overthinking their behaviors towards you and may be confused about how they're truly feeling. This uncertainty would cause you to dismiss your feelings in favor of thinking about them. This connection may be filled with guessing and speculations rather than knowing reality and seeing where they genuinely stand.

Conclusion

The best way to fix a one-sided relationship is to step away and focus on your self-worth and self-growth instead of trying to water a dead plant. You must focus on flourishing your own life instead of shifting your all to your partner. Your mental health should be your priority.